Basics

chain (ch)
1 Make a loop in the thread, crossing the ball end over the tail. Put the hook through the loop, yarn over the hook, and draw it through the first loop.
2 Yarn over the hook and draw through the loop. Repeat for the desired number of chain stitches.

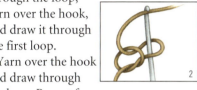

bead chain stitch (bcs)
1 Slide a bead against the base of the loop on the hook. Work a chain stitch.

single crochet (sc)
1 Insert the hook through the front and back of the first or second stitch from the hook. Yarn over and draw through the chain (two loops remain on the hook).
2 Yarn over and draw through both loops (one loop remains on the hook).

bead single crochet (bsc)
1 and 2 Before starting a single crochet, slide a bead against the base of the loop on the hook. Work normally.

slip stitch (sl)
1 Go into the next stitch as for a single crochet. Yarn over, and draw through the stitch and the loop.

double crochet (dc)
1 Yarn over. Insert the hook through the second stitch from the hook, yarn over, and draw through the stitch (three loops remain on the hook).
2 Yarn over and draw through two loops on the hook (two loops remain on the hook).
3 Yarn over and draw through the remaining two loops on the hook (one loop remains on the hook).

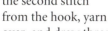

half-double crochet (hdc)
1 Yarn over. Insert the hook through the first or second stitch from the hook, yarn over, and draw through the stitch (three loops on the hook).
2 Yarn over and draw through all three loops on the hook (one loop on the hook).

bead double crochet (bdc)
1 Yarn over. Insert the hook through the second stitch from the hook, yarn over, and draw through the stitch (three loops remain on the hook).
2 Slide a bead against the base of the loop on the hook, yarn over and draw through two loops on the hook (two loops remain on the hook).
3 Yarn over and draw through the remaining two loops on

the hook (one loop remains on the hook).

treble crochet (tc)
1 Yarn over twice. Insert the hook through the second or third stitch from the hook, yarn over, and draw through the stitch. (four loops remain on the hook.)
2 Yarn over and draw through two loops (three loops remain on the hook).

3 Yarn over and draw through two loops (two loops remain on the hook).
4 Yarn over and draw through both loops (one loop remains on the hook).

join a ring
1 A slip stitch is used to join the first and last chains to form a ring. Insert the hook into the first stitch, going under the top part of the chain in the front and under the back loop.
2 Yarn over, and bring the yarn through both the stitch and the loop on the hook.

work into a ring
Insert the hook into the center of the ring, rather than into the chain stitch. Complete the stitch in the usual way. Work stitches into the ring, evenly spacing them around it.

half-hitch knot

Come out a bead and form a loop perpendicular to the thread between beads. Bring the needle under the thread away from the loop. Then go back over the thread and through the loop. Pull gently so the knot doesn't tighten prematurely.

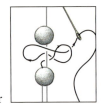

overhand knot

Make a loop and pass the working end through it. Pull the ends to tighten the knot.

surgeon's knot

Cross the right end over the left and go through loop. Go through loop again. Pull ends to tighten. Cross the left end over the right and go through once. Tighten.

lark's head knot

Fold a cord in half and lay it behind a ring, loop, bar, etc. with the fold pointing down. Bring the ends through the ring from back to front then through the fold and tighten.

knotting between beads

String all the beads for the strand before you begin knotting.

1 Loop the cord around the first three or four fingers of your left hand (right for lefties).
2 Pinch the cross between your thumb and index finger. Hold the cord circle open on your spread fingers with your palm up. Then drop the end of the cord through the circle into your hand.

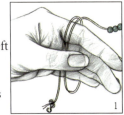

3 Put a long T-pin or an awl into the loop the same way the cord goes through. Gradually tighten the loop as it slips off your fingers, keeping the awl in it. Slide the awl toward the spot where you want the knot to be as you pull the bead end of the cord in the opposite direction. When the knot is right against the bead tip, let the cord slip off the tip of the awl. To set the knot, pull the two cord strands in opposite directions. Slide the next bead to the knot and repeat.

loops: opening and closing

1 Hold the jump ring with two pairs of chainnose pliers or chainnose and roundnose pliers, as shown.
2 To open the jump ring, bring one pair of pliers toward you and push the other pair away.
3 The jump ring is open. Reverse the steps to close.

loops: plain

1 Trim the wire or head pin ⅜ in. (10mm) above the top bead. Make a right angle bend close to the bead.
2 Grab the wire's tip with roundnose pliers. Roll the wire to form a half circle. Release the wire.

3 Position the pliers in the loop again and continue rolling, forming a centered circle above the bead.
4 The loop is complete.

wrapped loops

1 Make sure you have at least 1¼ in. (3.2cm) of wire above the bead. With the tip of your chainnose pliers, grasp the wire directly above the bead. Bend the wire (above the pliers) into a right angle.
2 Using roundnose pliers, position the jaws vertically in the bend.

3 Bring the wire over the top jaw of the roundnose pliers.
4 Keep the jaws vertical and reposition the pliers' lower jaw snugly into the loop. Curve the wire downward around the bottom of the roundnose pliers. This is the first half of a wrapped loop.

5 Position the chainnose pliers' jaws across the loop.
6 Wrap the wire around the wire stem, covering the stem between the loop and the top bead. Trim the excess wire and press the cut end close to the wraps with chainnose pliers.

Fringed scarf

This double crochet scarf is simple enough for beginners and combines sophisticated yarn with beautiful beads for an elegant look. Fringe and bead as described below. See "Basics," p. 3-4, for crochet stitches. Or, if you wish, you may achieve the same elegance by simply adding a beaded fringe to a purchased scarf—choose one with an edge that will be a good base for tying knots.

scarf

❶ With a size F hook, chain (ch) 45.

Row 1: double crochet (dc) in the fifth chain from the hook, then *ch 1, skip 1 ch, dc in the next ch**. Repeat from * to ** for 21 spaces.

❷ Row 2: ch 4, dc in the second dc, *ch 1, dc in the next dc**. Repeat from * to ** across 21 spaces. Repeat row 2 until the scarf is 44 in. (1.1m) long. Finish off. Refer to a basic crochet book for help if needed.

fringe

❶ To make 6-in. (15cm) fringes, cut 42 12-in. (30cm) strands of yarn. For each fringe, fold two strands in half and tie a lark's head knot in each of the spaces indicated on the drawing below.

❷ Cut eight 36-in. (.9m) strands of carpet thread. (This is longer than the fringe will be, but you'll use the excess length for knotting.) In the eight spaces indicated on the drawing below, tie on one doubled strand of carpet thread. String 15 beads on each pair of carpet thread strands, alternating between a group of three smaller beads and one rondelle as in the drawing. Tie an overhand knot after each bead (see "Basics" for instructions on knotting between beads). Leave ¼-½ in. (6-13mm) of space between groupings and knot before the first bead in each group. Seal the last knot with clear nail polish. When dry, trim the excess thread (detail photo above).

If you choose to fringe a purchased scarf instead of crocheting one, sew on ready-made fringe from the fabric store, or add your own with yarn or silk cord as described above. Tie on doubled carpet thread about ¼ in. from the bottom of the scarf. Begin about 1½ in. (3.8cm) from each edge and space the bead threads ½ in. apart as shown in the drawing. Bead and knot as described above. ○

– Gwen Blakely Kinsler

materials

- **2** 50gm skeins (300 yd.) double-knit yarn
- crochet hook, size F
- **240** 3-6mm glass beads and rondelles
- spool of carpet thread
- clear nail polish

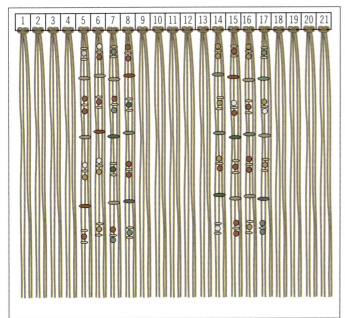

Beaded crochet band

This fancy crochet band is a small, portable, and versatile project—the 4½-in. (11.3cm) band can become a brooch or barrette with the addition of the appropriate finding. You can also turn the band into decoration for a guitar strap, a pet's collar, a day planner or scrapbook cover, or even salt and pepper shakers.

After crocheting the band with decorative yarn and crochet cotton, stiffen it, and then embellish it with wire, stone chips, ribbon embroidery, and beads – or any other decorative elements that appeal to you. If you are unfamiliar with the stitches, make a basic crochet band with plain yarn and thread and practice the embroidery stitches on scrap fabric with inexpensive ribbon and thread. See "Basics," pages 3-4, for crochet stitches.

making the band

❶ Use a size H hook and the fancy bulky yarn. Chain (ch)18.
❷ Double crochet (dc) in the third chain from the hook and in each of the remaining chains (15dc). Cut the yarn, leaving a 2-in. (5cm) tail, and pull it through the last loop to knot.
❸ Using a size 9 hook and #20 crochet cotton, pull up a loop in any stitch on one of the long sides of the strip (**photo a**). Make three single crochets (3sc) in each stitch on the long sides and 6sc on the ends. Slip stitch into the first stitch to join the end of the round to the beginning (**photo b**).
❹ Chain three, skip the first 2 sc on the previous round, and sc into the third (**photo c**). Repeat this step around. Slip stitch into the top of the first chain of the first 3ch.
❺ Work the following group of stitches in each 3ch space on the previous row to make an edging of small shells: sc, hdc (half double crochet), dc, hdc, sc. On the first 3ch loop at each end, work: sc, 3hdc, 3dc, 1tr (treble crochet). Work 1tr in the sc of the previous row at the center of each end. In the second 3ch space on each end, work: 1tr, 3dc, 3hdc, 1sc. When you get back to the start, slip stitch into the first stitch, cut the thread, and pull the tail through the last loop to knot it.
❻ To finish the base, iron it, then dip it in undiluted liquid starch. Let it dry flat. Don't begin embellishing before the starch is completely dry.

embellishing the band

❶ Cut a 12-in. (30cm) length of colored craft wire. Thread on one stone chip and bend the end of the wire behind the stone. Make a loop on top of the stone with roundnose pliers (**photo d**).
❷ Make a decorative loop between the first and second chips. Thread the second chip, make a loop on top of it, and repeat with five to eight chips for a piece that is ¼ in. (6mm) shorter than the fancy yarn center of the band (**photo e**). After making a loop on top of the last chip, bend the wire behind the chip to secure it. Clip the wire tails if necessary so they don't show on the front.
❸ Lay the wire and stone piece along the center of the band. Use beading thread and an embroidery needle to tack it in place with a few stitches close to the stones.
❹ Use the size 10 crochet cotton and an embroidery needle to fill in around the wire with French knots (**figure 1** at right and **photo f**). This step is optional but adds a lot of nice texture.

a

b

c

d

e

f

g

h

French knot

figure 1a

figure 1b

Figure 1a: Bring the thread out on the right side of the work. Wrap the embroidery yarn 2-3 times around the needle close to the fabric, wrapping toward the tail. Keep the wraps snug.

Figure 1b: Insert the needle as close to where the thread exits as possible but not in the same spot. Hold the knot with the thumb of your non-dominant hand until you've pulled the needle all the way through the fabric.

leaf stitch

figure 2a

figure 2b

Figure 2a: Come out on the right side of the fabric where you want the tip of the first leaf. Sew a diagonal stitch through the fabric at the base of the leaf. Sew diagonally on the wrong side, coming out at the tip of the other leaf of the pair.

Figure 2b: Sew back down into the same spot as the base of the first leaf.

❺ Anchor the green ribbon in an embroidery needle by threading it through the eye and then sewing through the ribbon tail near the end (**photo g**). Use it to make leaf-stitch pairs (**figure 2** at right) around each stone and in the loops between stones.

❻ Use bead thread and a #10 beading needle to space the crystals evenly across the piece. Then fill in randomly with the Japanese cylinder beads, three beads per stitch, close to the wire (**photo h**). Scatter more cylinder beads one at a time further out toward the crochet edging.

❼ Finally, anchor the flower-colored silk ribbon in the needle. Make a French knot rosebud in each pair of leaves that isn't next to a stone chip.

finishing

❶ Use bead thread to stitch all the thread ends down against the back of the piece.

❷ Sew or glue the piece to a pin finding, glue it to a barrette finding, or sew or glue it to anything else you want to decorate. ●

– Beth Boshears

materials

- 4⅓ yd. (4m) fancy yarn, worsted or bulky weight
- 20 yd. (18m) crochet cotton, #20
- 10 yd. (9m) crochet cotton, #10
- 3 yd. (2.7m) beading thread, Silamide or Nymo D
- crochet hooks, sizes H and 9 or sizes G and 8
- liquid starch
- 1 yd. (.9m) each silk ribbon, green and flower color, ⅛-in. (3mm) wide
- 1 ft. (30cm) 22-gauge colored craft wire
- assorted beads: **5-8** stone chips, **100-120** Japanese cylinder beads, **5-8** 3mm fire-polished beads
- needles: #10 beading, #18-20 and #24-26 embroidery
- barrette finding or long pin back finding
- E6000 glue

Tools: wire cutters, roundnose pliers

Optional: glue gun, hot glue

Beaded rope

Starting a crocheted rope can be frustrating if you don't have a knowledgeable companion nearby, so an easy, ladder-stitch alternative is also offered here. If you're comfortable with bead crochet, however, begin this necklace the traditional way. See "Basics," pages 3-4, for crochet stitches.

crocheting the rope

❶ Before you begin to crochet, transfer all the oval beads to upholstery thread. Tie the beads' temporary thread to the upholstery thread with a tight overhand knot (see "Basics," p. 4) and slide the beads across. Or, string the beads onto the upholstery thread using a Big Eye needle.

❷ Replace the Big Eye needle with a beading needle and work a four-bead ladder, as follows: Slide two beads to about 12 in. (30cm) from the tail end. Stitch through the second bead, going into the hole where the spool end of thread is exiting (**photo a**). Repeat, adding a third and fourth bead to the ladder in the same way.

❸ To connect the ladder into a ring, tighten the thread so the beads are parallel and sew through the first bead (**photo b**). Sew back through the fourth bead. Make one more pass through these two beads, then remove the needle. Hold the ladder so the thread tail exits the bottom and the working thread is at the top.

❹ Insert the crochet hook under the thread at the top of the bead that's closest to the working thread. Catch the working thread with the hook and bring it back under the bead's thread to form a loop (**photo c**, page 10). Working counterclockwise, insert the hook under the thread at the top of the next bead. (Lefties, work clockwise.) Slide a bead against the loop (**photo d**). Make a single crochet stitch.

❺ Continue to work counterclockwise around the ladder, making a total of four bead single crochet stitches in this row. The new beads will appear crowded and sit horizontally across the vertical beads in the ladder.

❻ Insert the hook between the bead and thread of the first bead added in the previous row. Push the bead to the right-hand side of the hook and pull up slightly on the hook (**photo e**). The bead, which was horizontal, will now stand up. Slide a new bead into place and make a single crochet. Repeat until your rope is the desired length. Keep the tension firm as you stitch and always bring down a bead before you make the first loop of each single crochet.

❼ Finish the rope by working a ladder of four beads into the last row of single crochet, so this end of the necklace will match the start. Or, stitch a row of single crochet (no beads) after the last row of beads.

❽ Cut the thread, leaving an 8-in. (20cm) tail. Knot the tail around the ladder threads or pull it through the last crochet loop to tie it off.

finishing the ends

You can either cover the end beads with bead caps and hide the thread in bullion wire or use bullion wire alone.

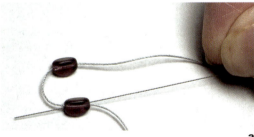
a

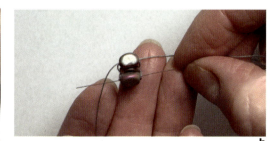
b

c

d

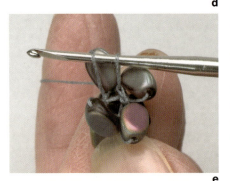

e

f

g

h

❶ If you're using bead caps, string a cap on each thread tail and slide it into place over the end beads.

❷ Cut a ½-in. (1.3cm) piece of bullion wire. Thread a needle onto one of the tails and go through the bullion (**photo f**). Avoid snagging the bullion as you slide it over the needle and thread and down to the rope.

❸ String half the clasp. Go back through the bead cap (if applicable) and into another bead in the end row. Pull the thread until the bullion nearly buckles to make a strong, neat loop around the clasp (**photo g**). Tie a half-hitch knot (see "Basics") to secure the thread in the beadwork. Repeat on the other end of the rope.

❹ Another way to finish the ends is to complete the bullion loop without stringing the clasp. Attach a jump ring and clasp after the loop is finished.

stringing the centerpiece bead

❶ Decide how you want to hang the focal bead. Tagua nut beads have openings in several places, which gives you a few options about position.

❷ Working with about 1 yd. (.9m) of Nymo, secure it in the beadwork near the necklace's center. Maneuver through beads and inside the rope, but don't allow any additional thread to show. Exit any bead near the center.

❸ String six to eight seed beads and go through the tagua bead. Check the tagua's placement and string another short run of beads. Go through a bead on the necklace rope. String more seed beads and repeat as necessary to support your focal bead (**photo h**).

❹ Create decorative tendrils along the crochet rope by stringing a few seed beads and sewing through a rope bead. Repeat randomly on both sides of the tagua bead. Secure the thread in the beadwork and trim the tail. ○

– *Sylvia Sur*

materials

- carved tagua nut bead (Red Horse Ranch, 949-831-1316)
- **300** 6mm oval 3-sided Czech beads
- 5g seed beads, size 10º or 11º
- clasp
- bullion wire, medium diameter
- Big Eye needle
- beading needles, #10 or 11
- Coats nylon upholstery thread
- Nymo D beading thread
- steel crochet hook, sizes 8-12

Tools: wire cutters
Optional: 2 bead caps

Bangle ensemble

Adding a wire core to a beaded crochet rope allows the rope to hold its shape and rest comfortably around your neck or wrist. This set's silver and lampwork beads add an appealing asymmetry to the design.

a

f

g

b

c

d

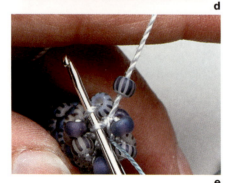
e

If this is your first bead crochet project, alternate two 6º bead colors when you string the beads in step 1. As you crochet, the beads will form a striped spiral pattern, and it will be easier to keep count and see where the next stitch is added. **Photos a-f** use two different bead colors so you can see how the beads lie at the beginning of the tube. See "Basics," pages 3-4, for crochet stitches.

crochet the tube

❶ Determine the length of the crocheted tube:

Bracelet: Temporarily string a bead cap, two silver beads, an art bead, and a bead cap on a wire or cord. Measure the length of the beads pushed close together. Add the length of the clasp (hook and jump or split ring) and ½ in. (1.3cm) for the loops. Subtract this number from the desired length of the finished bracelet for the length to crochet the tube.

Necklace: Temporarily string a bead cap, two silver beads, a large art glass bead, two silver beads, an art glass bead, and a bead cap on a wire or cord. Measure the length of the beads pushed together, and add ¾ in. (2cm) for the loops. Subtract this number from the desired length of the finished necklace.

❷ String all the seed beads on the cord. If you are still unsure of the length needed, string extra so you have enough beads. Do not cut the cord; leave it attached to the ball.

❸ Crochet six medium chain stitches and join the end to the beginning with a slip stitch (**photo a**).

❹ Position the hook so it goes through the two loops on the first stitch from the inside of the circle with the tip of the hook pointing out away from the circle.

❺ Slide the first bead down the cord to the crocheted circle. Catch the cord above the bead with the hook and make a slip stitch by pulling it through the stitch and the loop (**photo b**). One loop remains on the hook.

❻ Working counter-clockwise, insert the hook through the two loops of the next stitch in the circle. Slide a bead down the cord to the crocheted circle and make a slip stitch. Repeat until you have added six beads to the crocheted circle. The sixth bead will be stitched to the loop to the left of the tail (**photo c**). Notice how the beads lie sideways around the circle.

❼ Now you are ready to start the second row. This is the point where it is hard to see the next stitch. Insert the hook in the next loop, under the bead (**photo d**). Push the bead over the hook to the right. Bring the cord around the bead on the previous row so it is between the bead and the crocheted circle (**photo e**). Don't let the cord loop under the bead. Slide a new bead down the cord and make a slip stitch (**photo f**).

❽ Continue working around the circle until you have six beads on the second row. If you are alternating two colors, each color will line up above itself from row to row. The beads in the row below the working row will all sit straight with their holes in a vertical position.

❾ Crochet three or four more rows. Insert the 16- or 14-gauge wire from the bottom (under row 1) up through the center of the tube. As you crochet, keep the tip of the wire just above the row you are crocheting (**photo g**). If the wire slides out, gently try to work it back up through the tube, or pull out a few rows to get back to a point where you can push the wire up past the row you are working on.

❿ Continue crocheting around the wire until you reach the desired length.

⓫ Don't add beads to the last row of the crocheted tube. After the last row, cut the cord from the ball, leaving about a 4-in. (10cm) tail. Pull the tail through the loop to knot off.

finish the bracelet

❶ Hide the cord ends by tucking them inside the tube.

❷ String a bead cap, a silver bead, an art bead, and a silver bead on the wire (**photo h**).

❸ Make a loop at the end of the wire (see "Basics" and **photo i**).

❹ String a bead cap and a silver bead on the other end of the wire. Push the beads and the crocheted tube against the loop. Trim the wire so it is ½ in. past the last bead strung and turn a loop perpendicular to the first loop.

❺ Open the loop sideways (see "Basics" and **photo j**). Slide the loop through the jump ring on the clasp (**photo k**). Close the loop.

❻ Gently shape the bracelet into a circle with your hands. Start at the center of the bracelet and bend the ends in toward each other (**photo l**).

finish the necklace

The necklace can be modified to have a closure like the bracelet or to have a wire shape in the front. Just make sure the sides are balanced so the necklace hangs nicely.

❶ Crochet the tube for the necklace like the bracelet.

❷ Follow steps 1-3 for "finish the bracelet" to end one side.

❸ String a bead cap, a silver bead, a large art bead, and a silver bead on the other end of the wire.

❹ Push the beads and crocheted tube against the first loop and make a wrapped loop (see "Basics") above the last bead strung.

❺ Follow step 6 for "finishing the bracelet" to shape the necklace.

❻ Cut a piece of 20-gauge wire 2 in. (5cm) longer than the 16mm art bead and make a loop at one end of the wire.

❼ String a silver bead, the 16mm art bead, and a silver bead on the wire. Push the beads against the loop and make a second loop in the same plane as the first. Make three art bead links on 20-gauge wire.

❽ To finish the other end of the necklace, attach the bead links together so you have a chain of three bead links.

❾ Open an end loop on the bead chain and attach it to the loop on the plain end of the necklace. Close the loop. ●

– *Lynn Daniel*

materials

bracelet (8½ in./22cm, including clasp)
- 30-35g seed beads, size 6º
- 10 in. (25cm) 16- or 14-gauge sterling silver wire, dead soft
- **2** sterling silver bead caps (holes large enough to fit over 16- or 14-gauge wire)
- **3** 8-10mm sterling silver beads (holes large enough to fit over 16- or 14-gauge wire)
- art glass bead*
- sterling silver hook clasp with jump ring

necklace (17 in./43cm with a 2½ in./6.4cm dangle)
- 65-70g seed beads, size 6º
- 20 in. (51cm) 16- or 14-gauge sterling silver wire, dead soft
- 6-8 in. (15-20cm) 20-gauge sterling silver wire, half hard
- **2** sterling silver bead caps (holes large enough to fit over 16- or 14-gauge wire)
- **10** 8-10mm sterling silver beads (holes large enough to fit over 16- or 14-gauge wire)
- large art glass bead*
- **4** 16mm art glass beads*
  *(glass beads shown here by Gail Crosman-Moore)

both projects
- steel crochet hook, size 7
- ball #8 DMC pearl cotton or Conso cord to match seed bead color

Tools: roundnose and chainnose pliers, diagonal wire cutters

h

i

j

k

l

Double crochet bag

This little bag is so quick and easy you'll make one for everybody you know. Don't be put off by the term double crochet; it's very easy to do. As you crochet, the beads slide to the back of the piece, so ultimately, the wrong side becomes the right side.

String alternating color bead sets onto the DMC Metallic Pearl. Make a foundation chain, then complete each side of the bag in double-crochet stitches. Keep the tension even so the circular pieces don't become ovals. See "Basics," pages 3-4, for crochet stitches.

getting started
❶ Thread the end of the Metallic Pearl through a Big Eye needle. Do not cut the thread. String two color A beads, followed by two color B beads. Pick up alternating bead sets until you have strung a total of 70 sets.
❷ Make four chain stitches Join the chain into a ring with a slip stitch.

crochet the circles
❶ Chain one. Make a beaded chain stitch (**photo a**). Then make a second beaded chain stitch. This counts as the first double crochet. Remember, the beads slide to the back as you work.
❷ Make 13 beaded double crochet (bdc) into the foundation ring, spacing the stitches evenly around the ring. Connect to the first stitch with a slip stitch.

❸ Work the next row's first bdc as in step 1. Then make two bdc in each stitch of the previous row for a total of 28 stitches. **Photo b** shows the right side of the fabric; **photo c,** the wrong side. If the piece does not remain flat as you work, add an extra bdc as needed. Connect the last stitch to the first with a slip stitch.

❹ Work the next row's first bdc as in step 1. Make two bdc in the first stitch of the previous round. Then work one bdc in the next stitch. Repeat around the piece (**photo d**). If needed, work extra bdc so the piece remains flat. Connect the last and first stitches with a slip stitch.

❺ Repeat step 4 for the last row. Either work the pattern all the way around the piece to make a circular bag and end with a slip stitch, or leave 1½ in. (3.8cm) unworked to make the top edge. Leave a short tail and cut the thread. Weave in the tail.

❻ Repeat steps 1-5 to make the second side of the bag.

join the pieces

❶ Thread the Big Eye needle with 1 yd. (.9m) of Metallic Pearl. Anchor the tail in the fabric of the bag. Place the beaded sides together and sew through the first set of loops at the top edge of the bag (**photo e**). Thread a bead on the needle, then go through the loops on the other piece. Sew back through the bead (**photo f**).

❷ Repeat around the sides of the bag, leaving the top open.

❸ When finished, turn the bag inside out so the beaded fabric is exposed.

❹ Sew a decorative button or bead to the center front of the bag.

add the fringe

The bag at left features 13 beaded fringes that are worked along the bottom 1½ in. of the bag.

❶ Using 1 yd. of Silamide and a #10 needle, anchor the thread at the bottom center of the bag. String beads as shown in the **figure** at right.

❷ Repeat six times in one direction. Weave back to the center and repeat six times in the opposite direction.

❸ Tie off the tail and weave in the end.

make the neck strap

The neck strap for the bag is made with two strands of beads that occasionally pass through the same bead (see the strap of the bag at right). Use a random pattern of beads.

❶ Center a #10 needle on 5 ft. (1.5m) of Silamide. Anchor the doubled thread on one side of the first edge bead that joins the front to back. Thread a second needle and anchor it on the other side of the same bead.

❷ For 1-1½ in., string a matching selection of beads on each thread. Then pass both needles through one bead (as done with the large bead in the **figure**). Randomly string 28 in. (71cm) of beads in this manner.

❸ Anchor the ends of the strap in the opposite side of the bag as in step 1. ●

– Sandy Amazeen

materials

- 15g size 8º seed beads, color A
- 15g size 8º seed beads, color B
- assorted beads for strap and fringe
- DMC Metallic Pearl crochet thread, size 5, silver or gold
- button or bead for front side
- crochet hook, size D
- Big Eye needle
- beading needles, #10
- Silamide to match bead color

figure

c

d

e

f

Crocheted bead purse

Purse frames, both antique and contemporary, can inspire the creation of beautiful vintage-style purses like these. For the larger purse at left, use an antique silver frame and size 9º 3-cut seed beads. The smaller purse (directions below) uses a Lady Delight #2 frame about 4 in. (10cm) wide (other frames up to about 5 in./12.7cm will also work), Champion silk (Gudebrod) size 2 or 3 or FF, and size 9º 3-cuts. You can also use size 11º seed beads and up to #8 DMC perle cotton. These purses were crocheted with a size 10 (1.3mm) steel hook, but if you use thicker thread or crochet tightly, you'll want to use a larger hook, up to size 7 (1.5mm).

Since sliding beads over the thread can abrade it quickly, string about two strands of beads at a time and knot the newly strung thread to the completed work at the edge of a row. If the thread is slippery, dot the knots with clear nail polish or glue. If your beads have smooth, large holes, you can string three to four strands at a time.

After crocheting the purse front and back, cut out the lining and sew it together. Next sew the crocheted purse together. Then insert the lining in the purse and sew the pieces to the purse frame. Add trim over the lining where it is sewn to the frame if desired. Finally, crochet and attach the handle. See "Basics," pages 3-4, for crochet stitches and abbreviations.

crocheting the purse

The first row of crochet is easy because the beads face away from you. Working the second row with the beads facing you is trickier, requiring a slight twist of the wrist, shown and explained in **photos a-c.**

❶ If your thread is thin enough and your bead holes large enough, thread a Big Eye needle with the end of the silk or cotton thread. Working directly from the hank, thread on the desired number of beads. If the thread is too thick to allow the beads to pass over two thicknesses, stiffen the end with clear nail polish and twist it into a tight point while the polish is still tacky. Use the stiffened end of thread as a needle.

❷ To start crocheting: ch73, make 2ch, turn.

Row 1: In the 3rd ch from the hook, sc. Sc in each stitch (st) to the end; 1ch, turn.

Row 2: 1sc in each sc of previous row; 1ch, turn.

Row 3: 1bsc, 1sc. Repeat this pattern to the end of the row; 1ch, turn.

Row 4: 1sc in first sc, *1bsc, 1sc*. To crochet with the beads on the side facing you, slip the bead down to the work and insert the hook into the stitch below behind the bead (**photo a**). Catch the thread by putting the hook over, rather than under, the thread and pull through the loop on the hook behind the bead (**photo b**, page 18). Yarn over and pull through both loops to complete the sc (**photo c**). Repeat *-* to end; 1ch, turn.

Rows 5-25: Repeat rows 3 and 4. If you want to make the purse longer than about 7 in. (18cm), repeat rows 3 and 4 for the desired extra length, ending with a row 3.

Row 26: With the right side facing, 1sc; then 1bcs in each stitch until the one before the end (keep the beads facing the right side of the work), 1sc; 1ch, turn.

Row 27: Repeat row 26 (beads will be on the side away from you).

Rows 28-29: 1sc in each sc of previous row; 1ch, turn.

Row 30: This is where you begin the star pattern. 1sc in each of the first 6 sc. *1bsc, 5sc, 1bsc, 11sc*. Repeat *-* until last 6sc, 1 sc in each; 1ch, turn.

a

b

c

d

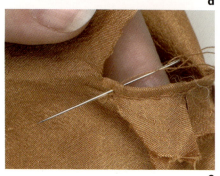
e

f

g

h

Row 31: 1sc in first 6 sc. *2bsc, 3sc, 2bsc, 11sc*. Repeat *-* until last 6 sc, 1sc in each; 1ch, turn.

Row 32: 1sc in first 6 sc. *3bsc, 1sc, 3bsc, 11sc*. Repeat *-* until last 6 sc, 1sc in each; 1ch, turn.

Rows 33-35: Repeat row 32.

Row 36: 1sc in first 5 sc. *3bsc, 3sc, 3bsc, 9sc*. Repeat *-* until last 5 sc, 1sc in each; 1ch, turn.

Row 37: 1sc in first 3 sc. *3bsc, 7sc, 3bsc, 5sc*. Repeat *-* until last 3 sc, 1sc in each; 1ch, turn.

Rows 38-39: Repeat row 37.

Row 40: Repeat row 36.

Rows 41-44: Repeat row 32.

Row 45: Repeat row 31.

Row 46: Repeat row 30.

Rows 47-48: sc in each sc to the end of the row; 1ch, turn.

Row 49: 1sc; then bsc in each stitch to 1 stitch before the end, 1sc; 1ch, turn.

Row 50: Repeat row 49, but do not make 1ch; turn at the end of the row.

Row 51: This is where you decrease the width of the crocheted fabric to leave room for the hinge of the purse frame at each edge. Sl st over the first 6 sc, 1ch, *1bsc, 1sc*, repeat *-* to the last 6 sc before the end of the row; 1ch, turn **(photo d)**.

Rows 52-66: 1sc in each of first 2 sc, *1bsc, 1sc*; repeat *-* to the end; 1ch, turn. Repeat until the length of this section matches the depth of the frame above the hinge.

Rows 67-70: 1bsc in first sc, *1sc, 1bsc*; repeat *-* to the last st; end 1sc, 1ch, turn.

Rows 71-72: On these rows, decrease to shape the fabric into the top of a curved frame: *3sc, skip 1 st*; repeat *-* across the row. If the top is straight, work these rows without decreases or beads. End the thread.

❸ With the wrong side facing, pick up along the bottom edge, working 1 row of sc; 1ch, turn. Work the second side from rows 2-72.

lining

❶ Trace around the crocheted piece on paper. Add ½-in. (1.3cm) seam allowances around the outside **(figure)**. Cut out a lining piece including the seam allowances.

❷ Clip the seam allowance diagonally at all four **point A**s to just shy of the sewing line.

❸ Fold the lining at the center bottom and sew the side seams from **points B-C**.

❹ Press the top of the side seam allowance open and fold the clipped area above the side seam down over the seam. Tack it in place with small hand stitches **(photo e)**.

assembly

❶ Sew the side seams of the crocheted piece from the bottom to the top of the wide section.

❷ Pick up all around the top and open sides and work a row of sc, decreasing length as necessary to fit the frame. You'll gather the width to fit, which will allow enough fullness so the purse can open all the way.

❸ Sew an accent bead to the center of each of the stars, if desired.

❹ Slip the lining inside the crocheted bag with the seams against each other.

❺ Run a gathering thread across the top of each side and adjust each to the width of the pierced top of the frame.

❻ Use doubled sewing thread to sew through the holes on the frame, joining the lining and crochet on each side of the frame edge. Sew a bead over the holes on the crochet side as you join the pieces to keep the outside neat and the beading consistent all the way to the top **(photo f)**.

MEGA SHARKS

picthall and gunzi

an imprint of Award Publications Limited

ISBN 978-1-909763-34-0

First published 2019

Copyright © 2019 Picthall and Gunzi, an imprint of Award Publications Limited
The Old Riding School, Welbeck, Worksop, S80 3LR

All rights reserved. No part of this publication may be reproduced, stored in a retrieval system or transmitted in any form or by any means, electronic, mechanical, photocopying, recording or otherwise, without the prior written permission of the copyright owner.

Written and edited by: Nina Filipek
Designed by: Jeannette O'Toole

Images: Page 4: *Dwarf lantern shark* – Dr Gregory R. Mann; all other images: Shutterstock (front cover: *Great white shark* – Willyam Bradberry, *Background* – Dudarev Mikhail; page 1: *Great white shark* – Mogens Trolle; page 3: *Whale shark* – Krzysztof Odziomek, *Blacktip reef shark* – Eric Isselee, *Nurse shark* – frantisekhojdysz, *Great white shark with seal* – Sergey Uryadnikov, *Mermaid's purse* – B. Speckart, *Bull shark head shot* – Willyam Bradberry, *Great white shark* – Joe Belanger, *Scalloped hammerhead shark* – Matt9122, *Blue shark* – Dray van Beeck, *Whale shark* – Krzysztof Odziomek, *Angel shark* – Stephen Nash, *Grey reef shark* – Willyam Bradberry, *Megalodon* – Catmando, *Shark fin soup* – 54613, *Leopard shark skin* – Christophe Rouziou; pages 4–5: *Background* – Rich Carey, *Whale shark* – Krzysztof Odziomek, *Caribbean reef shark* – VisionDive, *Leopard shark* – Aleksandr Sadkov, *Blacktip reef shark head shot* – zebra0209; pages 6–7: *Blacktip reef shark* – Eric Isselee, *Dorsal fin* – Jamen Percy, *Great white shark* – Jim Agronick, *Tail shot* – Sergey Uryadnikov; pages 8–9: *Background* – littlesam, *Nurse shark* – frantisekhojdysz, *Great white shark* – Stefan Pircher, *Six gill shark* – Greg Amptman, *Nurse shark with coral* – Matt9122; pages 10–11: *Great white shark* – Mogens Trolle, *Whale shark feeding* – Dudarev Mikhail, *Great white shark with seal* – Sergey Uryadnikov, *Tiger shark* – Matt9122, *Sand tiger shark* – MP cz; pages 12–13: *Young white shark* – Petra Christen, *Great white shark* – kbrowne41, *Young dogfish* – Susana_Martins, *Mermaid's purse* – B. Speckart; pages 14–15: *Background* – Willyam Bradberry, *Bull shark* – Willyam Bradberry, *Bull shark head shot* – Willyam Bradberry, *Bull shark feeding* – Willyam Bradberry, *Bull shark and divers* – Ciurzynski; pages 16–17: *Great white shark* – Jim Agronick, *Great white shark head shot* – Elsa Hoffmann, *Tooth* – BW Folsom, *Great white shark white belly* – VisionDive, *Seals* – Erwin Niemand, *Dolphins* – TAGSTOCK1, *Turtles* – Rich Carey, *Other sharks* – Fiona Ayerst; pages 18–19: *Background* – Rich Carey, *Scalloped hammerhead shark* – Matt9122, *Stingray* – Kristina Vackova, *Hammerhead shark close-up* – Matt9122, *Great Hammerhead shark* – Shane Gross; pages 20–21: *Blue shark* – Dray van Beeck, *Shoal of tuna* – Rich Carey, *Blue shark and boat* – Joost van Uffelen, *Blue shark from below* – Brandelet, *Squid* – Narchuk, *Anchovy* – evantravels, *Lobster* – Ethan Daniels, *Shrimp* – Bennyartist; pages 22–23: *Whale shark* – Krzysztof Odziomek, *Diver* – fenkieandreas, *Whale shark front on* – Krzysztof Odziomek, *Whale shark with remora fish* – Soren Egeberg Photography, *Plankton* – Johnlips, *Jellyfish* – pan demin, *Krill* – Dmytro Pylypenko; pages 24–25: *Background* – Vilainecrevette, *Angel shark* – Stephen Nash, *Flounder* – Beth Swanson, *Angel shark skin* – Stephen Nash, *Leopard shark* – Christophe Rouziou; pages 26–27: *Background* – littlesam, *Coral* – Jolanta Wojcicka, *Reef shark* – frantisekhojdysz, *Group of blacktip reef sharks* – Dray van Beeck, *Grey reef shark* – Willyam Bradberry, *Pink coral* – Le Do, *Angel fish* – serg_dibrova; pages 28–29: *Background* – Rich Carey, *Megalodon* – Catmando, *Megalodon tooth* – Jake Kohlberg, *Great white shark tooth* – BW Folsom, *Megalodon silhouette* – Catmando, *Man silhouette* – Vector Goddess, *Megalodon feeding* – Catmando; pages 30–31: *Great white shark* – Mogens Trolle, *Whale shark* – Krzysztof Odziomek, *Scalloped hammerhead shark* – Matt9122, *Shark fishing* – Emmanuel R Lacoste, *Shark fin soup* – 54613, *Angel shark* – Stephen Nash, *Great white shark* – Joe Belanger, *Background* – littlesam)

Please note that every effort has been made to check the accuracy of the information contained in this book, and to credit the copyright holders correctly. Picthall and Gunzi apologise for any unintentional errors or omissions and would be happy to include revisions to content and/or acknowledgements in subsequent editions of this book.

19 1

Printed in China

CONTENTS

What Is a Shark? 4

Shark Parts 6

Shark Senses 8

Shark Diet 10

Shark Pups 12

Bull Shark 14

Great White Shark 16

Hammerhead Shark 18

Blue Shark 20

Whale Shark 22

Masters of Disguise 24

Reef Sharks 26

Prehistoric Shark 28

Save Our Sharks! 30

Glossary 32

WHAT IS A SHARK?

Sharks are an amazing group of fish, found in all the oceans of the world. They have been around since before the dinosaurs. Today, there are over 400 types, or species, of shark, from the tiny dwarf lantern shark (16 centimetres long) to the gigantic whale shark (up to 12 metres long).

Can you spot the dwarf lantern shark?

Whale shark

Dwarf lantern shark

Huge mouth

Weighs 18,700 kilograms and is as long as a school bus

Eye

Fishy!

Sharks are fish. They have a smooth, pointed body shape, which is good for swimming, and a tail and fins for steering their way through the water.

Caribbean reef shark

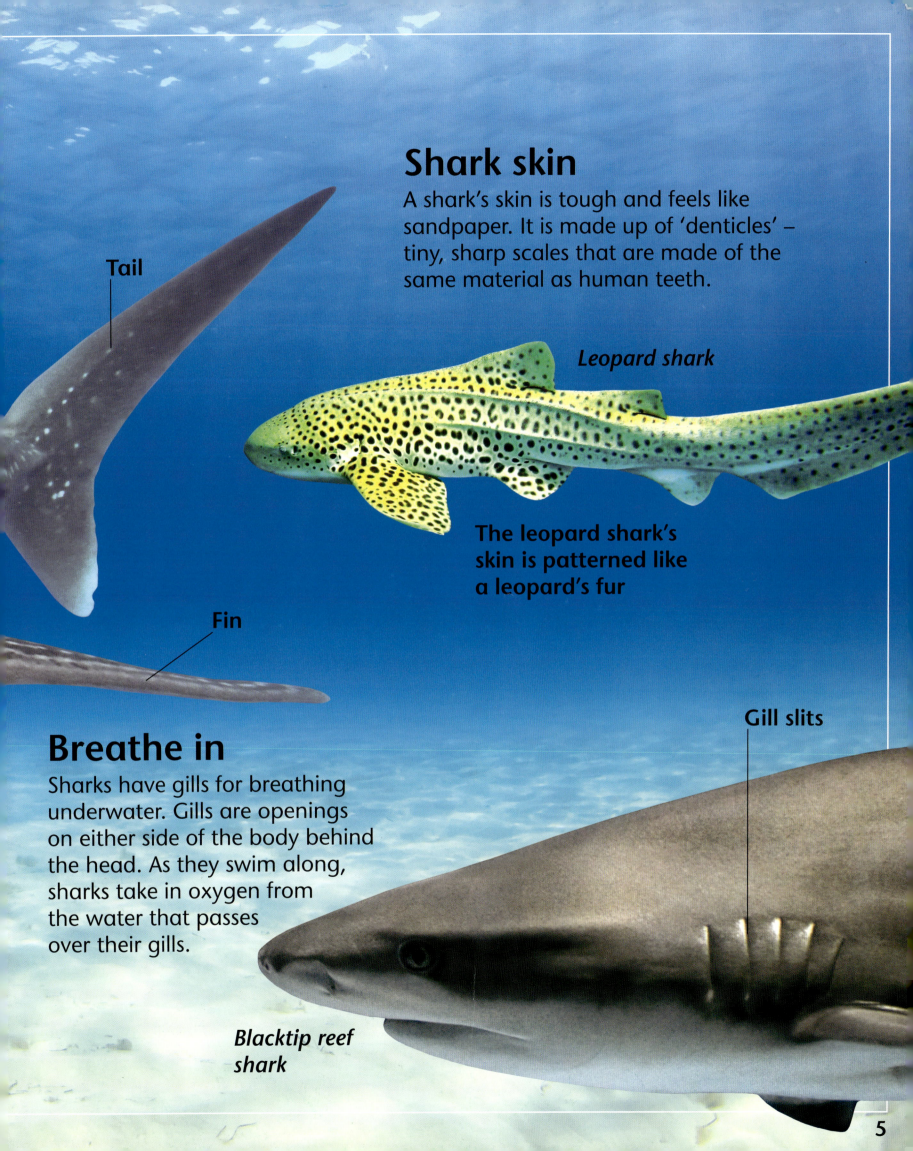

Tail

Shark skin
A shark's skin is tough and feels like sandpaper. It is made up of 'denticles' – tiny, sharp scales that are made of the same material as human teeth.

Leopard shark

The leopard shark's skin is patterned like a leopard's fur

Fin

Gill slits

Breathe in
Sharks have gills for breathing underwater. Gills are openings on either side of the body behind the head. As they swim along, sharks take in oxygen from the water that passes over their gills.

Blacktip reef shark

SHARK PARTS

Unlike many other fish, sharks don't have bony skeletons. Their skeletons are made up of a light, bendy material called 'cartilage' – it is similar to the material that makes up your ears and nose. This allows sharks to move with ease and speed.

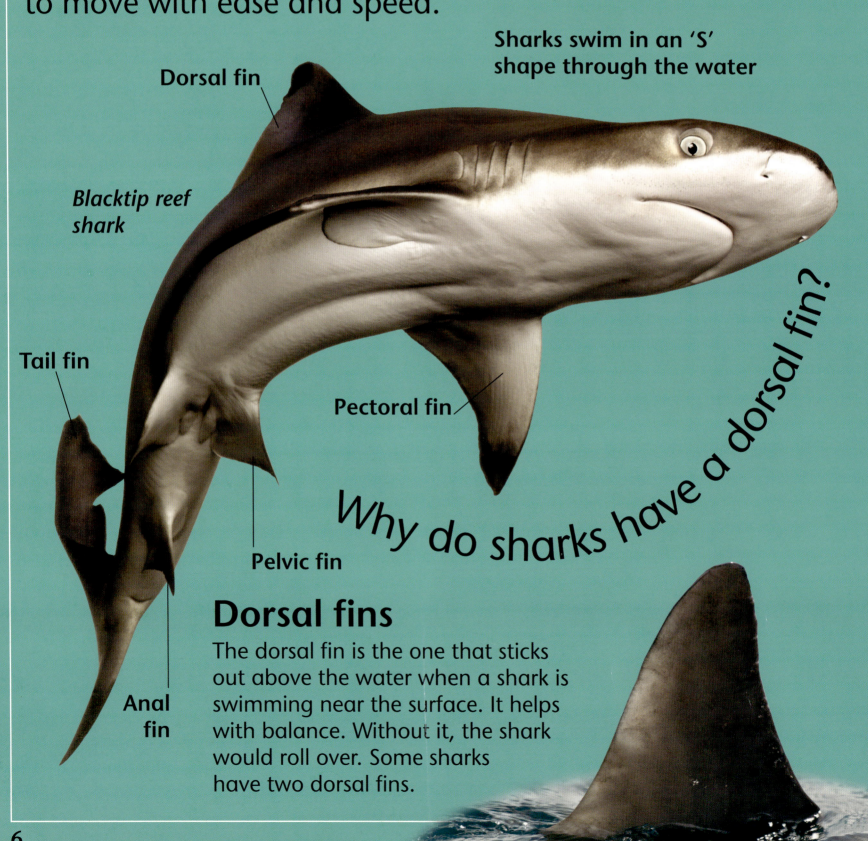

Sharks swim in an 'S' shape through the water

Dorsal fin

Blacktip reef shark

Tail fin

Pectoral fin

Pelvic fin

Anal fin

Why do sharks have a dorsal fin?

Dorsal fins
The dorsal fin is the one that sticks out above the water when a shark is swimming near the surface. It helps with balance. Without it, the shark would roll over. Some sharks have two dorsal fins.

Great white shark

Pectoral fins
The two pectoral fins under the body are used for steering and to lift the shark in the water as it swims.

Pectoral fins

Tail fins
The tail fin moves from side to side as the shark swims, and is important for generating power and speed in the water.

Great white shark

Can you point to?

a dorsal fin

teeth

a tail

SHARK SENSES

All sharks have an excellent sense of smell and most have very good eyesight. They can smell their food, or prey, and detect movement in the water from a great distance away. Most sharks' eyes are on either side of their head so they can see all around – except directly in front of their nose!

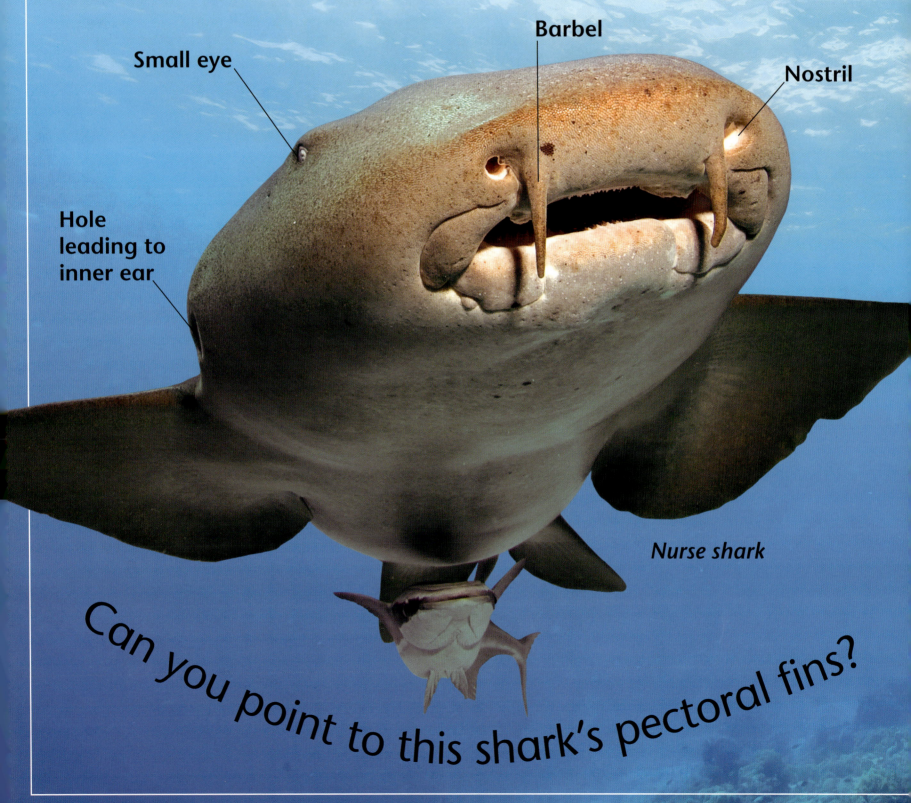

Small eye

Barbel

Nostril

Hole leading to inner ear

Nurse shark

Can you point to this shark's pectoral fins?

Nosey!

A shark's nostrils are not used for breathing – just for smelling! The great white shark can smell the blood of an injured fish from half a kilometre away! It does this using sensors inside the nostril slits – also called 'nares' – on either side of its nose.

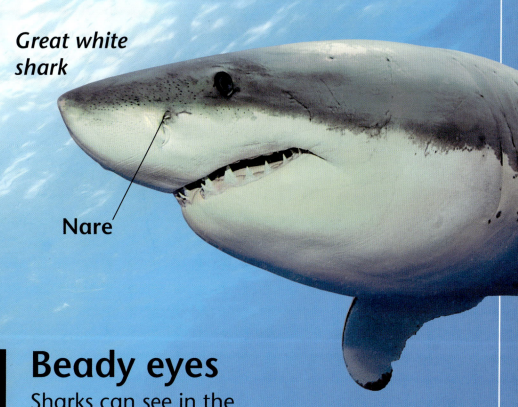

Great white shark

Nare

Beady eyes

Sharks can see in the water much better than we can. Most sharks have eyelids that they can half close to protect their eyes if they are attacked, or when they are feeding.

Sixgill shark

Nurse shark

Barbel

Barbels

Nostril barbels look like fleshy whiskers. They are used to feel and taste prey on the ocean bed.

SHARK DIET

Sharks are fierce hunters of other fish in the sea. As well as eating fish, the bigger sharks will eat sea turtles, seals and penguins. However, some of the biggest sharks feed on the smallest of sea creatures, called 'plankton'.

What does this shark eat?

Great white shark

Razor-sharp teeth

Filter feeder

The whale shark swims with its huge mouth wide open, scooping up plankton as it goes.

Great white shark

Surface attack
Great whites push their prey up to the surface as they attack. But this great white fails to catch a seal meal this time!

Huge appetite
The tiger shark has been called the 'garbage can of the sea' because it will eat anything and everything. It has a massive appetite, and may swim for more than 40 kilometres a day in search of food.

Petrol cans, car tyres and baseballs have all been found in the stomachs of tiger sharks!

Tiger shark

Terrible teeth
Sharks are famous for their sharp teeth. Sand tiger sharks have three rows of sharply-pointed teeth, which curve backwards, to help them hold on to their prey.

Sand tiger shark

SHARK PUPS

Baby sharks are called 'pups'. Most hatch from eggs inside the mother shark, then continue to grow and develop inside her until they are born. Mother sharks swim to safer waters, such as lagoons, to give birth, as the pups are left to look after themselves from the moment they are born.

What is a baby shark called?

White shark pup

The young shark is a miniature version of the adult

Can you point to?

 an eye

 spotted skin

 sharp teeth

Adult great white shark

Shark pups
Some types of shark have only a few pups, but many will have around 10. On average, only two out of a litter of 10 pups will survive and grow into adult sharks.

Mermaid's purse
While most sharks give birth to live pups, some sharks, such as dogfish, lay eggs. Inside this egg case (called a 'mermaid's purse') there is a shark's egg. The shark grows inside and hatches after about six months.

Tendrils attach to seaweed

Mermaid's purse

Young dogfish

BULL SHARK

The bull shark is one of the most dangerous to humans as they often swim in warm waters by the shore. It can also live in fresh water, so can swim up rivers too. They eat mainly fish but also turtles and other sharks, and some even attack hippos in rivers!

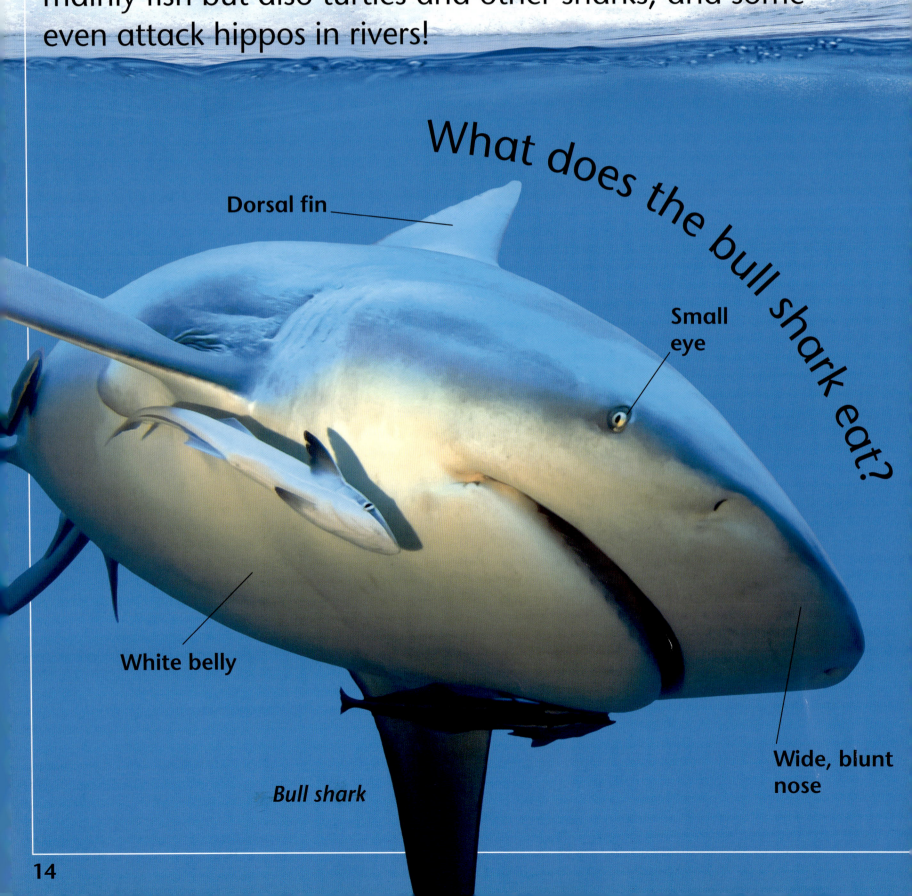

Dorsal fin

What does the bull shark eat?

Small eye

White belly

Bull shark

Wide, blunt nose

Can you point to?

a diver

an eye

a dorsal fin

Poor eyesight

The bull shark usually hunts in murky waters where it can swim without being seen easily. It uses its good sense of smell to find its prey.

It has smaller eyes than most other sharks

Bump and bite

Because these sharks can't see very well, they tend to bump into their prey first before they bite!

Bull shark feeding in the Pacific Ocean

Short and stocky

Bull sharks can grow up to 4 metres long and weigh as much as 230 kilograms. However, it is wider and shorter than the great white.

The divers are keeping a safe distance from this bull shark

GREAT WHITE SHARK

One of the world's largest and most famous sharks is the great white. You may have heard about these sharks attacking people, but this is rare. When sharks attack people, it is because they mistake them for their usual prey, such as whales, dolphins, seals and other fish.

Why does it have sharp teeth?

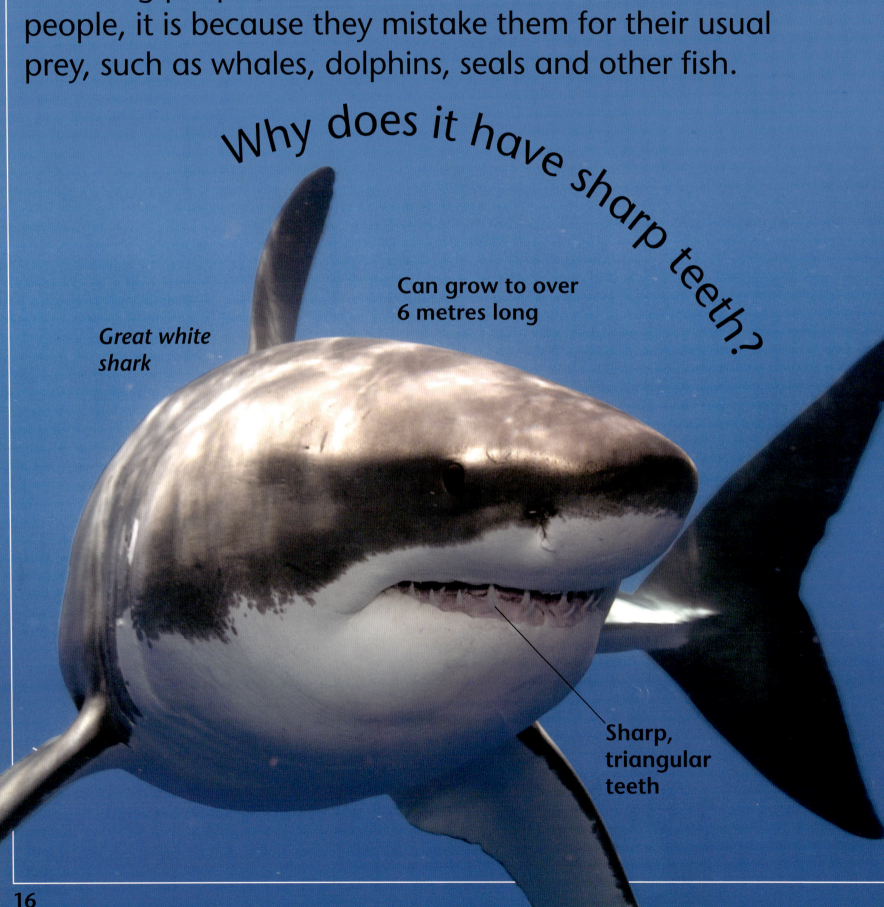

Great white shark

Can grow to over 6 metres long

Sharp, triangular teeth

Jaws!

Great whites can have up to 30,000 teeth in their lifetime. When they lose a tooth another one moves forward to take its place.

Actual size

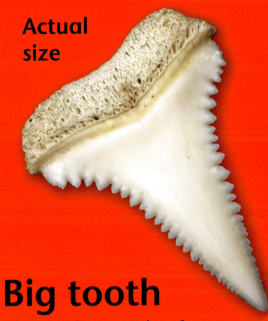

White belly

The great white shark is actually grey and white. It has a white belly, but its body is grey on top so that it is not seen when swimming underneath prey.

Big tooth

This is the tooth of a great white. It grows up to 7.5 centimetres long. Even the sides of the tooth are sharp and jagged.

Grey colour on top

White belly

Great white shark's diet

seals

dolphins

turtles

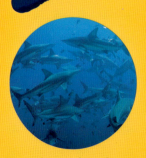
other sharks

HAMMERHEAD SHARK

It is easy to see why this shark is called a hammerhead! Scientists think the unusual shape of its head helps the hammerhead to spot its prey. The eyes, set on each side of its head, give it a wide view of the sea all around.

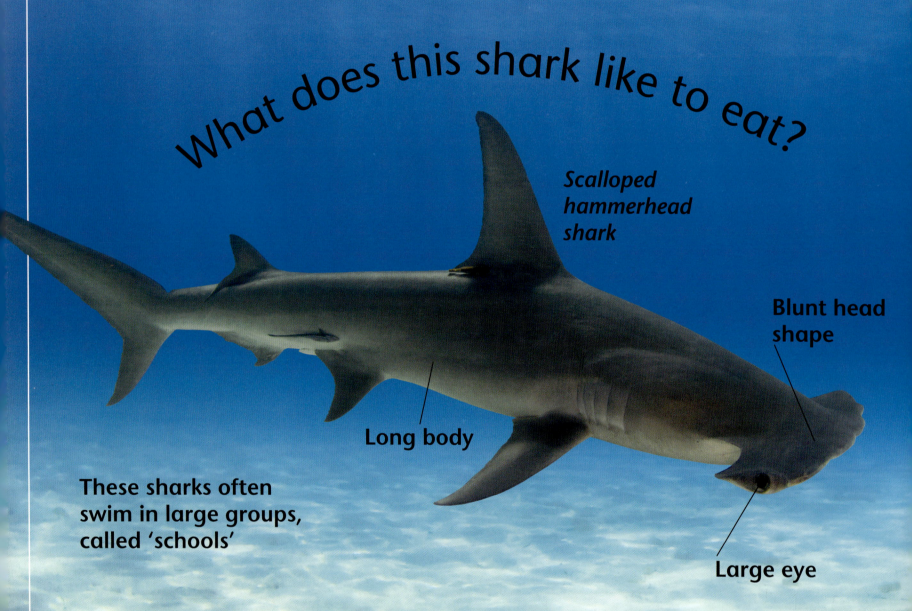

What does this shark like to eat?

Scalloped hammerhead shark

Blunt head shape

Long body

Large eye

These sharks often swim in large groups, called 'schools'

Hide and seek

Why do you think this bluespotted ribbontail ray is hiding in the sand? Because the hammerhead shark likes to eat them!

Keeping cool

Hammerhead sharks are found in warm seas throughout the world. But in the hot summer months, they often swim to cooler waters.

Can you point to?

an eye

teeth

stingray

Great hammerhead

Most hammerhead sharks are small, but the largest – the great hammerhead shark – can grow up to 6 metres long.

Great hammerhead shark

BLUE SHARK

This shark is one of the fastest swimmers in the sea. When chasing prey, it reaches speeds of up to 40 kilometres per hour. Known as the 'wolf of the sea', the blue shark travels many thousands of kilometres each year across the world's oceans.

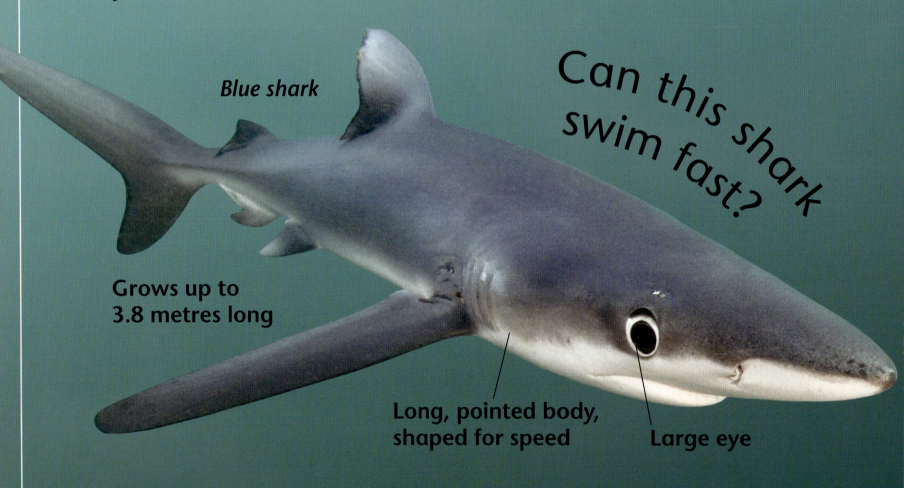

Blue shark

Can this shark swim fast?

Grows up to 3.8 metres long

Long, pointed body, shaped for speed

Large eye

Fast food

These sharks will eat smaller fish, such as tuna or anchovy, by swimming straight through the middle of the shoal with an open mouth. They eat as many as they can catch while on the move!

A shoal of small tuna

This blue shark is swimming underneath a boat!

Midnight feast

The blue shark prefers cooler waters and is most often found in the deeper parts of the North Atlantic. For some of the year, it moves to shallower waters at night, where food is more plentiful, in order to feed.

Deeper waters are cooler

Can you point to?

a squid

an eye

tuna fish

Blue shark's diet

squid anchovies lobsters shrimps

WHALE SHARK

The whale shark is the biggest shark in the world, and grows up to 12 metres in length. It is harmless to humans as it only feeds on tiny animals and its 300 teeth are only about 3 millimetres long. Despite their huge size, whale sharks are generally friendly, and even let scuba divers swim close by.

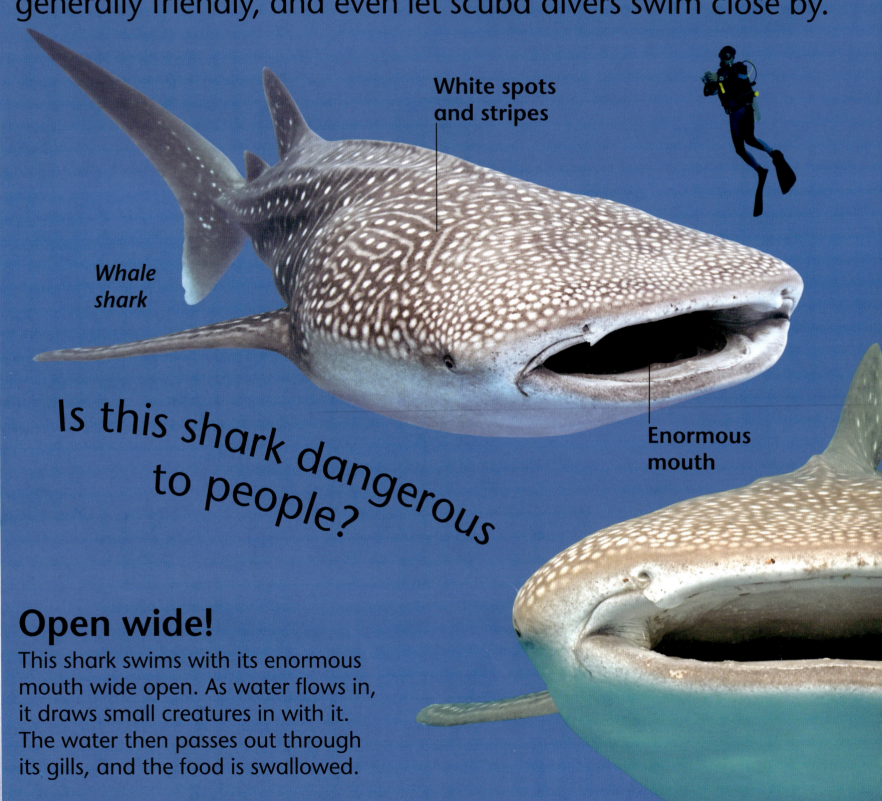

White spots and stripes

Whale shark

Enormous mouth

Is this shark dangerous to people?

Open wide!
This shark swims with its enormous mouth wide open. As water flows in, it draws small creatures in with it. The water then passes out through its gills, and the food is swallowed.

Can you point to?

an eye jellyfish remora fish

In the fast lane

A shoal of remora fish is hitching a ride in the whale shark's slipstream. Remoras can use a sucker on their head to attach themselves to the whale shark.

Whale shark's diet

plankton jellyfish krill

MASTERS OF DISGUISE

The angel shark has a flattened body and pectoral fins that extend from its body, which look a little like an angel's wings. It only grows to about 2 metres long at most. Its teeth are tiny triangles, but they are as sharp as needles!

Can you see its nose barbels?

Fin shaped like a wing

Flattened body

Angel shark

Colour camouflage

The angel shark's skin colour matches the sand on the sea bed, to fool its prey and to help it hide from other, fiercer sharks. This is called 'camouflage'.

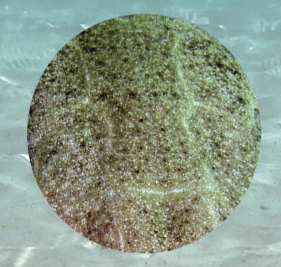

Flounder are the prey of the angel shark

Hidden danger

The angel shark buries itself in the sand on the ocean bed. With only its eyes peeping out, it waits for passing prey, such as flounder or halibut. Then it darts quickly upwards, attacking from below.

Leopard shark

Though its body is not as flat as the angel shark, the leopard shark also uses camouflage to hide on the ocean floor as it hunts its prey.

Leopard shark

REEF SHARKS

Sharks that live in the shallow tropical waters around coral reefs are called reef sharks. These include the whitetip, blacktip, grey and Caribbean reef sharks.

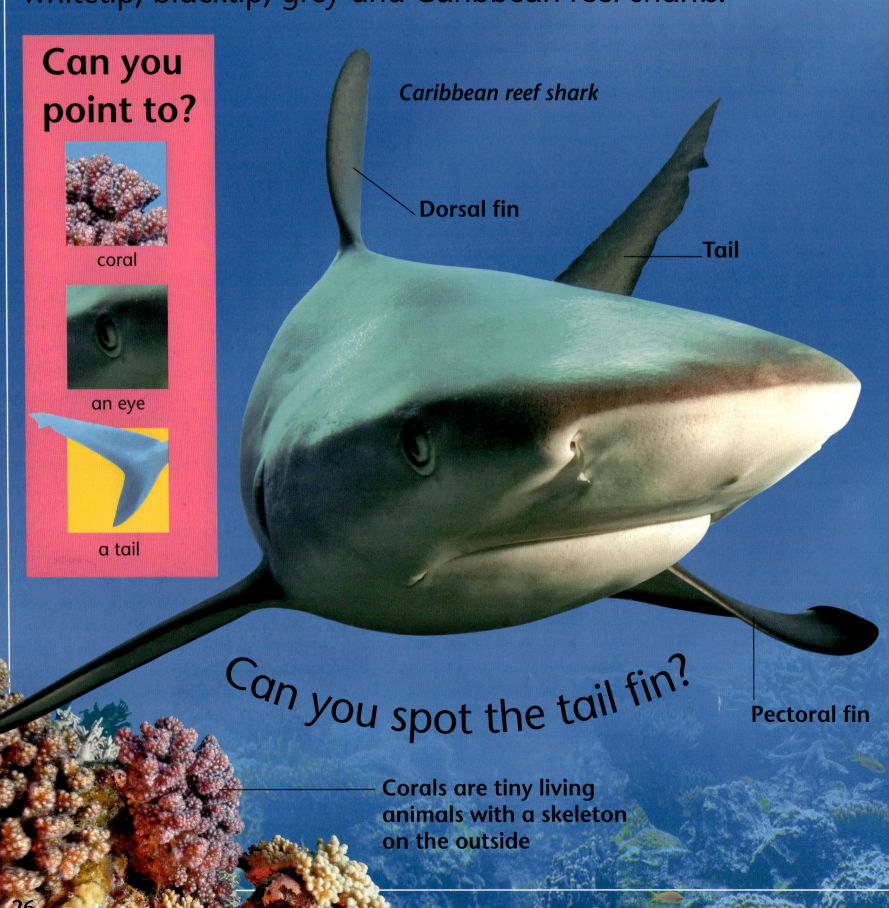

Can you point to?
- coral
- an eye
- a tail

Caribbean reef shark

Dorsal fin

Tail

Can you spot the tail fin?

Pectoral fin

Corals are tiny living animals with a skeleton on the outside

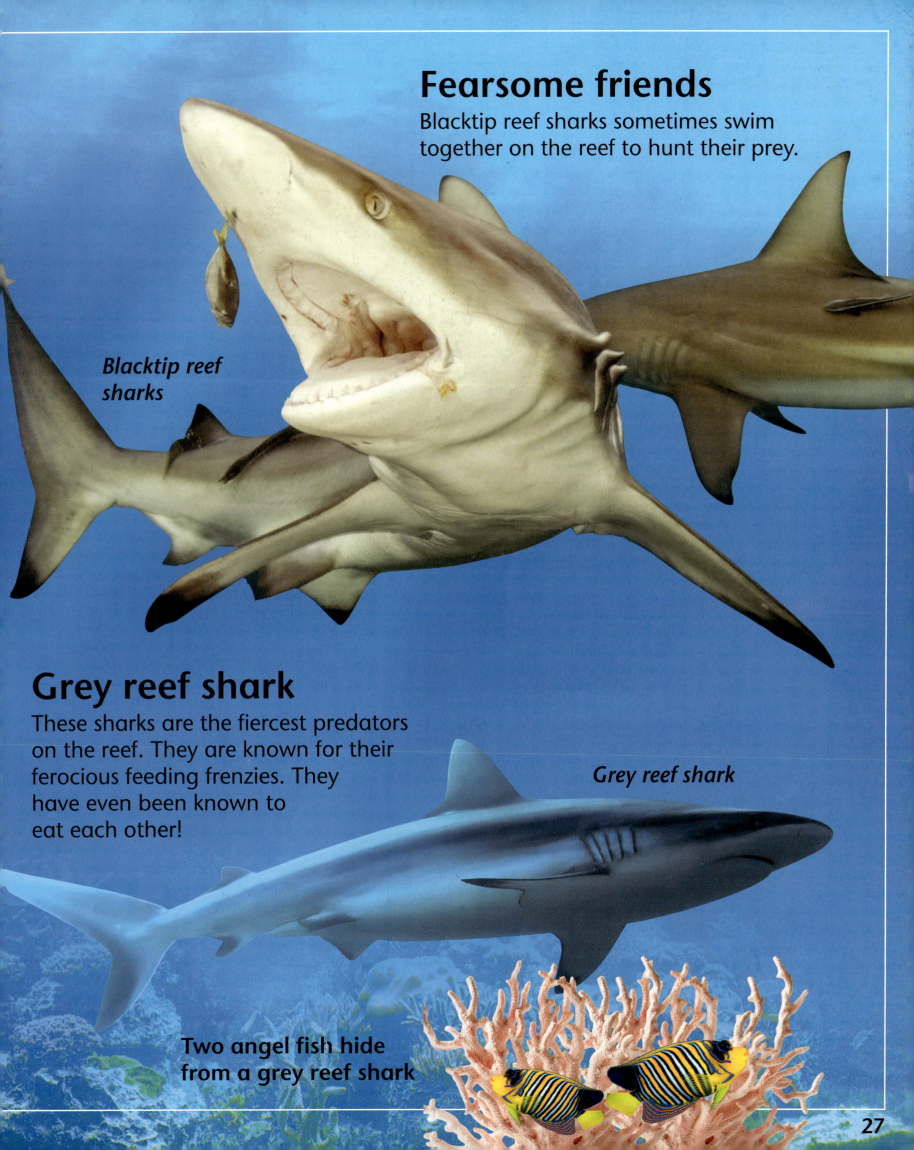

Fearsome friends
Blacktip reef sharks sometimes swim together on the reef to hunt their prey.

Blacktip reef sharks

Grey reef shark
These sharks are the fiercest predators on the reef. They are known for their ferocious feeding frenzies. They have even been known to eat each other!

Grey reef shark

Two angel fish hide from a grey reef shark

PREHISTORIC SHARK

One of the biggest and most powerful sharks that ever lived was called megalodon. Its name means 'giant tooth'. This shark is now extinct, but in prehistoric times it would have ruled the oceans. Megalodon's closest living relative is the great white.

What do you think it might have eaten?

Huge jaws

Dagger-like teeth

Megalodon

Powerful body

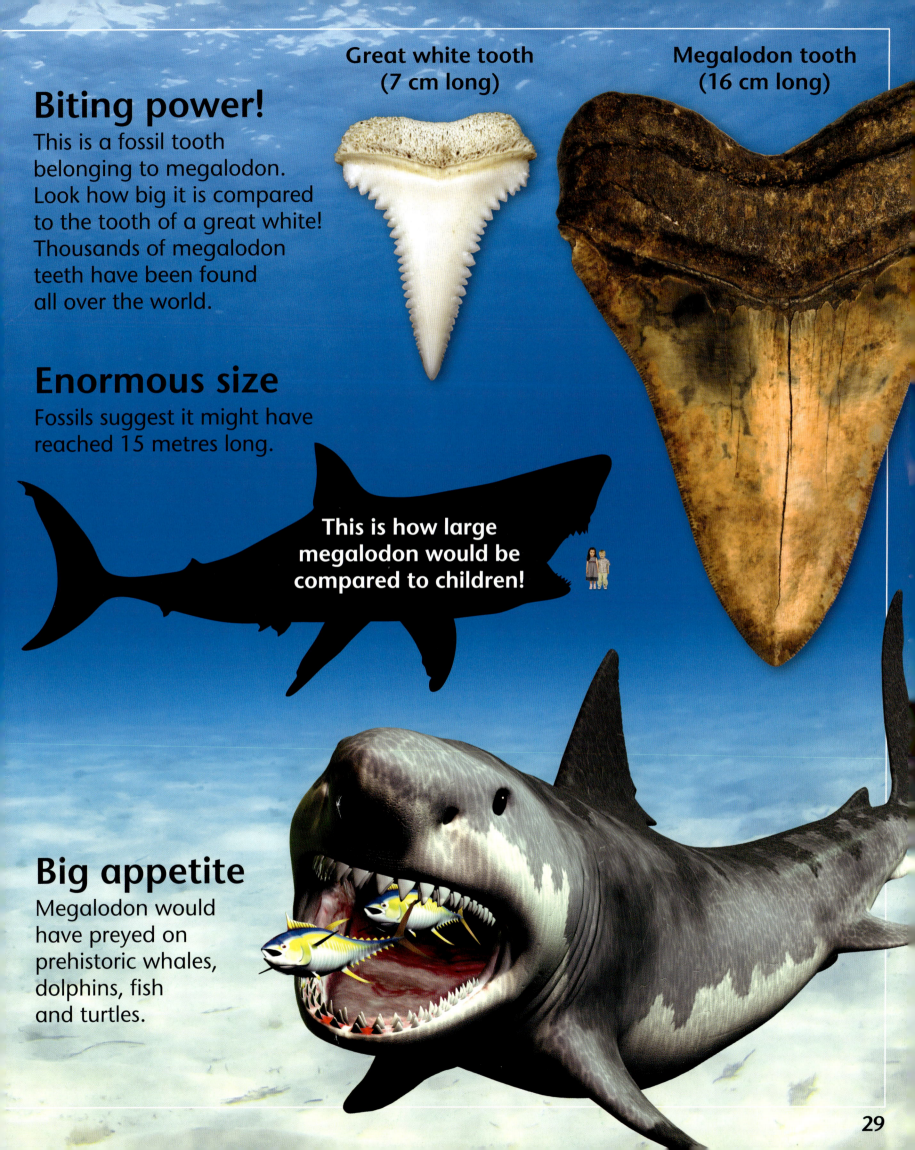

Biting power!

This is a fossil tooth belonging to megalodon. Look how big it is compared to the tooth of a great white! Thousands of megalodon teeth have been found all over the world.

Great white tooth (7 cm long)

Megalodon tooth (16 cm long)

Enormous size

Fossils suggest it might have reached 15 metres long.

This is how large megalodon would be compared to children!

Big appetite

Megalodon would have preyed on prehistoric whales, dolphins, fish and turtles.

SAVE OUR SHARKS!

The survival of many types of shark is now threatened by human activity, such as fishing and changes to their habitat (where they live). Some are caught by accident and some are hunted for their body parts, such as the jaws of great whites, which can be sold for high prices.

Great white shark

Jaws

The numbers of whale sharks and scalloped hammerhead sharks are falling

Fishing kills over 100 million sharks each year

Extinction

Many young sharks are being killed before they have had a chance to have pups. This means some species may be threatened with extinction and could disappear from our oceans.

Shark soup

Many sharks are now in danger from people who catch them for sport or food – either for meat or to make shark fin soup.

Unhealthy sea

The sea is becoming an unhealthy place for sharks. The pollution of the oceans and the destruction of coral reefs damage the habitats that sharks need to live, feed, breed and grow.

Once common in waters around Europe, the angel shark is now critically endangered

What can we do?

Now we know that sharks are amazing animals, we need to do all we can to protect them!

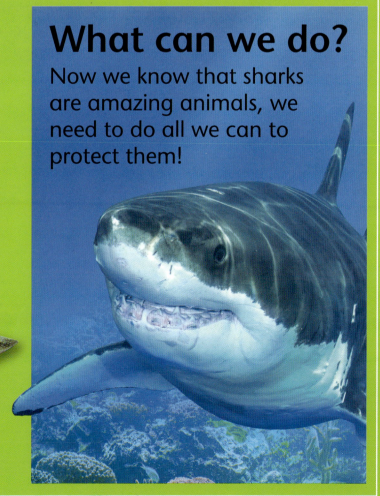

GLOSSARY

Barbel – a fleshy 'feeler' that gows from the mouth or snout of a fish.

Camouflage – a pattern on an animal's skin that helps it to blend in with its surroundings.

Cartilage – firm but flexible tissue in the body. Human ears are made of cartilage.

Dorsal – positioned on the back or upper side of an animal.

Extinct – an animal or plant becomes extinct when all of its kind have died. Once that happens, the species is lost for ever and cannot be brought back to life.

Kilogram – 1000 grams. The same approximate weight as a litre of water, or an average pineapple.

Kilometre – 1000 metres, or about the length of 11 soccer pitches.

Pectoral – positioned on the chest area of an animal.

Plankton – tiny ocean animals and plants that make up the food for many larger animals.

Predator – an animal that hunts other animals.

Prehistoric – from a long, long time ago, before anything was written down.

Prey – an animal that is hunted by another animal.

Slipstream – a position around or behind a moving object, where it is easier for another object to follow, because the object in front moves the air or water out of the way.

Species – a group of animals or plants that are so similar that the males and females can have babies together.

GUESS WHO?

Study the pictures. Can you name the sharks shown here?

Whose teeth are these?

Whose skin is this?

Whose mouth is this?

Whose nose is this?

Look back through the book to see if you were right.